PENGUI

THE SQUA

Ronald Searle was born in ᴜ studied art there before serving ᴀ ᴀ ᴛ ᴜᴇ army – half of them as a prisoner-oᴛ war of the Japanese. After his release in 1945, he began freelancing from London and was soon contributing to publications all over the world. Ronald Searle has published some fifty books, either alone or in collaboration. Since 1961 he has lived in France.

RONALD SEARLE

THE SQUARE EGG

PENGUIN BOOKS

Penguin Books Ltd, Harmondsworth, Middlesex, England
Penguin Books, 625 Madison Avenue, New York, New York 10022, U.S.A.
Penguin Books Australia Ltd, Ringwood, Victoria, Australia
Penguin Books Canada Ltd, 2801 John Street, Markham, Ontario, Canada L3R 1B4
Penguin Books (N.Z.) Ltd, 182–190 Wairau Road, Auckland 10, New Zealand

—

First published in Great Britain by Weidenfeld & Nicolson 1968
First published in the United States of America
by The Stephen Greene Press 1968
Published in Penguin Books 1980
Copyright © Ronald Searle, 1961, 1962, 1963, 1964, 1965, 1966, 1967 and 1968
The following nine drawings appeared originally in
the *New Yorker*: page 6 and 40 (1966); pages 12, 14, 16,
40, 53, 88 and 92 (1967). Copyright ©
The New Yorker Magazine, Inc., 1966, 1967
All rights reserved

—

Made and printed in Great Britain
by Hazell Watson & Viney Ltd,
Aylesbury, Bucks

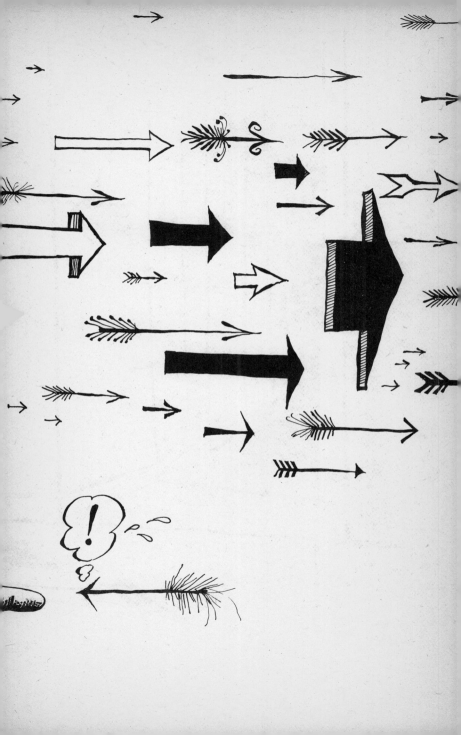

Ronald Searle

ronald searle

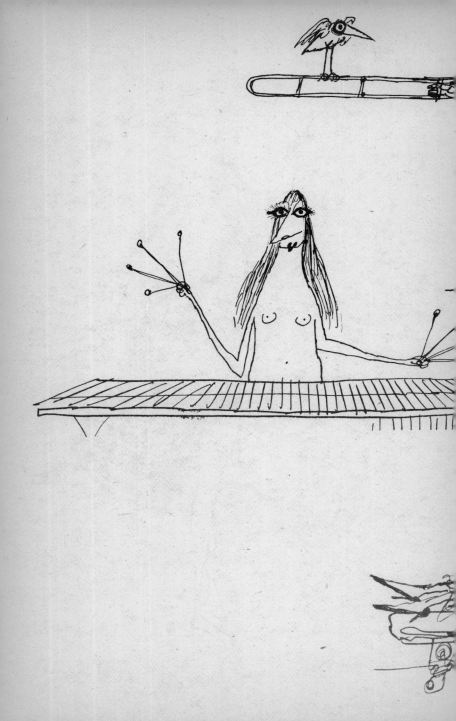

Ronald Searle

Ronald Searle

Ronald Searle

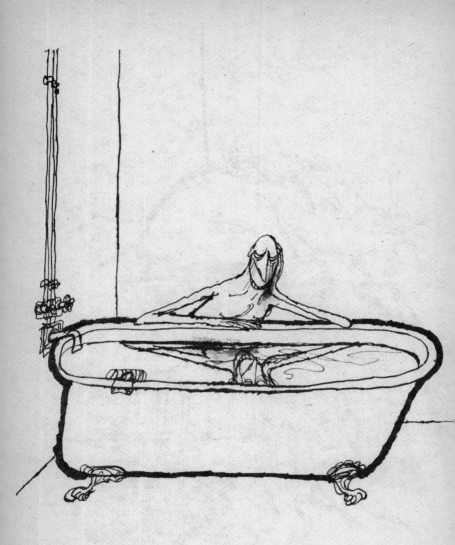

Ronald Searle

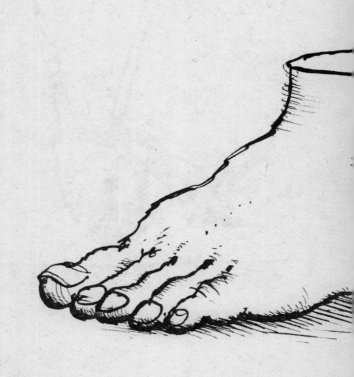

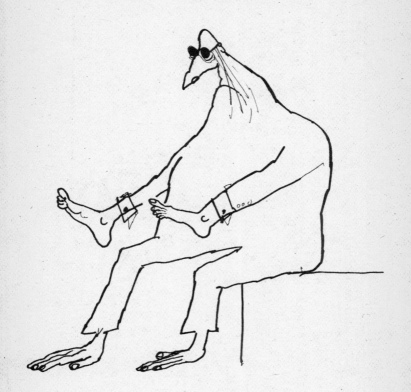

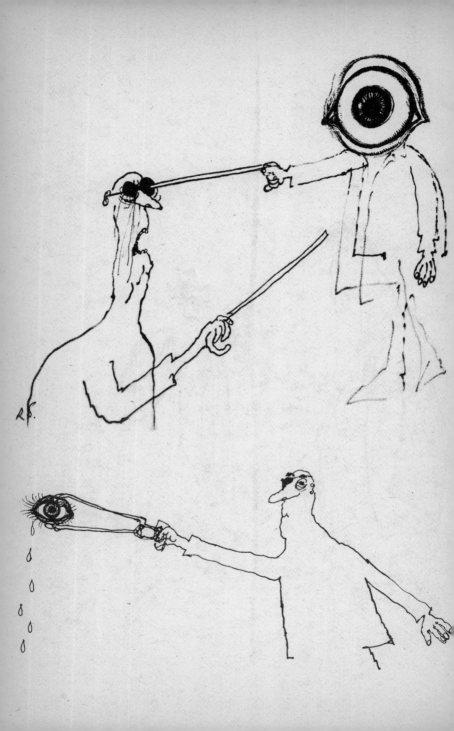

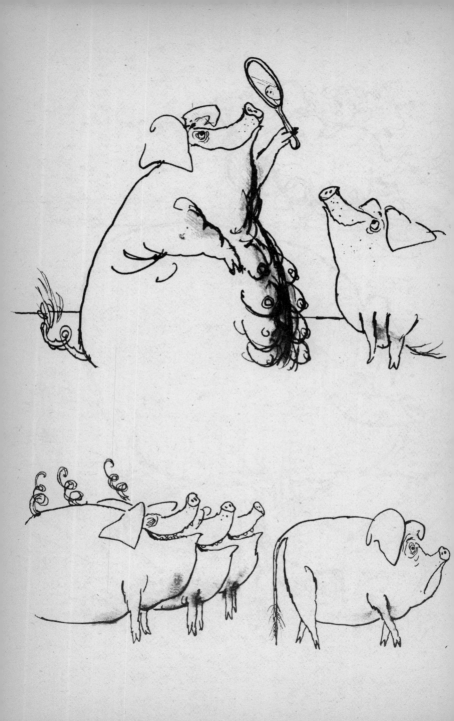

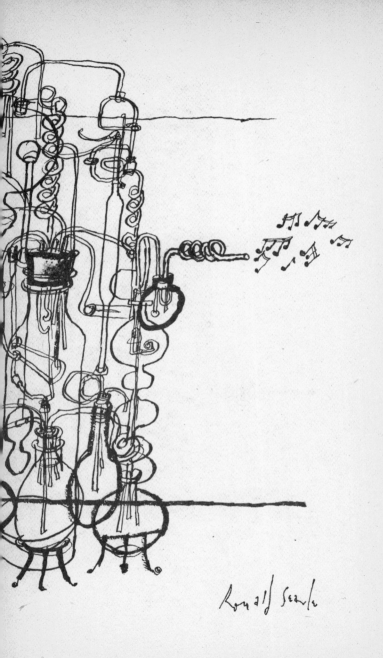

Ronald Searle

Graffiti

Ronald Searle

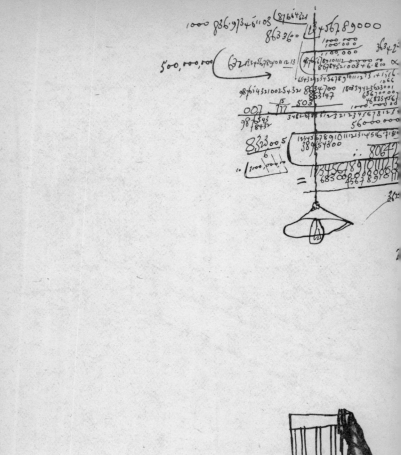

Ronald Searle

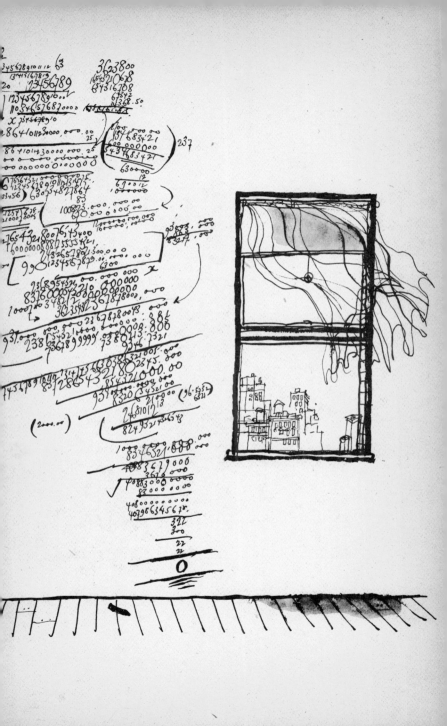